WELCOME TO DRYBURGH ABBEY

Of all the great abbeys in the Scottish Borders, Dryburgh has the most dilapidated church – only the transepts survive nearly intact – but the best preserved cloister. The medieval buildings of the east range are in good condition, though the upper floor was adapted in the late 1500s to accommodate a commendator's house.

The setting seems tranquil today, but like the neighbouring abbeys at Melrose, Jedburgh and Kelso, Dryburgh suffered repeatedly in wars that raged across the Borders, especially in the 1300s and 1500s. Before the Protestant Reformation of 1560, both abbey and town were already in terminal decline.

It was not until 1786 that David Steuart Erskine, 11th Earl of Buchan, acquired the abbey run by his ancestors and revived the romantic appeal of these ruined buildings.

Above: A carving of *Agnus Dei* ('The Lamb of God'), originally part of a ceiling boss, and now on display in the parlour.

CONTENTS

EXPLORE

The abbey church	4
The nave and choir	6
The presbytery	7
The transepts	8
The cloister	10
The east range: upper floor	12
The east range: ground floor	13
The chapter house	14
The warming house and the novices' day room	15
The south range	16

HISTORY

The history of Dryburgh Abbey	18
The abbey's foundation	20
The early years of the abbey	22
The Premonstratensians	24
The daily round	26
War and peace	28
The later years	30
Buchan's romantic ruin	32
Sir Walter Scott	34
Earl Haig and after	35
DISCOVER HISTORIC SCOTLAND	36
HISTORIC SCOTLAND MEMBERSHIP	37
FURTHER READING	37

DRYBURGH ABBEY AT A GLANCE

Widely considered to be the most beautiful of the Border abbeys, Dryburgh Abbey occupies a picturesque bend in the River Tweed which has been carefully landscaped and planted to complement the ruins.

Founded in the mid-1100s, Dryburgh was the first Premonstratensian abbey in Scotland. Its first canons came from Alnwick in Northumberland. Although the abbey never aspired to the wealth and political influence enjoyed by the neighbouring abbeys at Jedburgh, Kelso and Melrose, it now offers visitors one of the finest locations in which to appreciate the contemplative, spiritual lives of medieval canons. It also reveals some very fine examples of ecclesiastic architecture and stonemasonry.

The abbey's location near the border with England resulted in devastating attacks by English armies, beginning in 1322. A sustained attack in 1544 proved to be the final blow, from which the abbey never recovered. Thereafter, the abandoned abbey was enjoyed first as a private home, then as a romantic ruin and garden. It is the burial place of David Erskine, Sir Walter Scott and Field Marshal Earl Haig.

AT A GLANCE

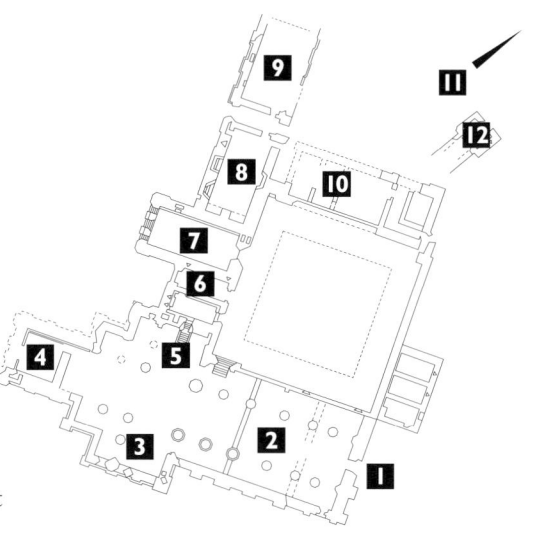

1 WEST DOOR
Rebuilt following a devastating raid in 1385, the west door would once have been part of a grand façade, probably dominated by a large window.

2 NAVE
The space used by lay people attending services, flanked by aisles. Little survives apart from the bases of the pillars.

3 NORTH TRANSEPT
The best-preserved part of the church, rising to almost its full height and now the setting for the graves of Walter Scott and Earl Haig.

4 PRESBYTERY
The church's most sacred area at its east end, housing the high altar. It would have been highly decorated though little evidence survives.

5 SOUTH TRANSEPT
Only the grand south gable now survives of a structure that would have mirrored the north transept.

6 PARLOUR
A small room where the canons were allowed to converse, now housing a display of finely carved masonry.

7 CHAPTER HOUSE
The most important room of the cloister, where the community assembled daily for meetings and readings.

8 WARMING HOUSE
A heated chamber where canons could briefly enjoy the benefit of a fire.

9 NOVICES' DAY ROOM
A substantial room where recently recruited canons underwent training.

10 SOUTH RANGE
Little survives of the refectory, or dining room, that occupied the upper floor. The vaulted chambers below still stand.

11 OBELISK
A curious feature of the abbey grounds, erected in 1794 in honour of the abbey's founder Hugh de Moreville.

12 GATEHOUSE
Added in the 1500s to provide a point of arrival to the commendator's house.

DRYBURGH ABBEY

THE ABBEY CHURCH

The abbey was built on a site that slopes gently down towards the south, so the main buildings were constructed on a series of partly artificial terraces. The church, being the most important building, occupies the highest ground. Although much of it has not survived, it remains a fine example of Gothic architecture.

Dedicated to St Mary the Virgin, the church consists of a nave, north and south transepts with chapels protruding from their eastern walls, and a rectangular presbytery. In plan it is shaped like a stepped cross. A bell tower once rose over the crossing, and we must be thankful that when it collapsed it did not demolish the north transept, which remains the finest hint of what has been lost. Judging by the number and size of the surviving windows, the church was unusually well lit for a building of its period.

Construction work began in the latter half of the 1100s, but most of what survives dates either to the early 1200s, or to the rebuilding following the abbey's destruction by Richard II of England in 1385.

Top left: The south transept viewed through the west door of the abbey church.

Left: Canons entering the church from the cloister via the processional doorway.

EXPLORE

THE WEST DOOR

The church is entered through the west door, which is round-headed, heavily moulded and decorated with blocks, each ornamented with stylised leaves. To either side are buttresses, and beyond them lancet windows. The façade above the door probably contained a large window featuring ornate stone tracery. All of the west end of the church dates to the rebuilding after 1385.

A small graveyard to the north of the church contains a notable group of memorials to tenants and staff of the Dryburgh estate, dating from the 1600s and 1700s.

Right: The west façade of the church. Although it has suffered severe damage, it would once have been magnificent and imposing, probably with a large window above the doorway.

THE MERELLES BOARD

The north wall of the church provides a fascinating insight into the daily life of the masons who built it. Crudely scratched onto a stone is a board (left) used by the men to play the game of merelles or 'nine men's morris'. This is a game for two players in which each attempts to place three counters in a line, thus gaining one of the opponent's counters. Very few examples have been found in Scotland and all are associated with monastic houses. Another fine example is on display at Jedburgh Abbey.

THE NAVE AND CHOIR

The nave was used by the lay folk of the district for worship. At the west end of the north wall are the remains of a doorway. This would have been the normal entrance into the church for lay people attending services; the west door would have been used only on high days and holy days.

So little of the nave survives that any reconstruction would be largely conjecture. However, there is evidence at the junction of the north aisle and the west wall that the aisles flanking the nave were vaulted over in stone. Each aisle was separated from the central part of the nave by an arcade of six pillars and one engaged pillar on the inner face of the west wall.

At the east end of the south wall are two piscinae, stone basins used for rinsing altar vessels after the celebration of Mass. These offer evidence that this area at least was divided into small chapels where the canons offered up private prayers for their benefactors.

The nave was closed off from the canons' own choir by a pulpitum or screen wall. This was located on the line of the second piers west of the crossing. Only its foundations survive, including the centrally-placed doorway. The canons' choir lay at the heart of the abbey. The choir-stalls stretched from the pulpitum eastward across the central crossing and beneath the bell tower to the presbytery at the east end.

The brethren spent the greater part of their day in the church and their stalls would doubtless have been beautifully carved and of the highest quality, reflecting the importance of this part of the church.

Top: The north and south transepts seen from the nave.

Above left: The choir seen from the east, with the south transept at the left and the north transept at the right.

THE PRESBYTERY

Located at the east end of the church, beyond the canons' choir, the presbytery housed the high altar. As in the nave, so much has been lost that accurate description is not possible.

On the evidence of the surviving north wall, the north and south walls probably each had three lancet windows, and it is likely that the east wall continued the theme. Below the windows, there are slight traces of arcading around the lower walls. This appears to have taken the form of engaged, intersecting arches supported on short pillars, similar to those in the east wall of the chapter house (see illustration, page 14).

Initially, the high altar, the main focus of the canons' worship, was probably placed against the east wall. A variety of furnishings would have been provided nearby, to enhance the setting for the celebration of Mass. At a later stage, the high altar appears to have been relocated a little further west against a screen, the stone footings of which remain. The space behind the screen may have been a chapel, perhaps housing a revered reliquary – a case to hold holy relics.

Below: The presbytery, where the high altar would have stood. The gravestones inserted into its walls were added after the abbey fell out of use.

DRYBURGH ABBEY

THE TRANSEPTS

To the north and south of the central crossing were the transepts, or cross-arms, of the church, projecting beyond the nave aisles. These provided additional space, mainly for chapels for private devotion.

The main roofing of the transepts, in common with the nave and presbytery, was of timber set at a steep pitch. The chapels projecting from the east of the transepts were vaulted over in stone.

The north transept is the more complete and much of its carving is as crisp as it was when completed. The north gable, now largely gone, had two tiers of three lancet windows, each similarly decorated inside and out; the elevations around the west and south sides of the chapels are of an elegant, three-storeyed design. Above the pointed arches leading into the chapels is a shallow triforium, or gallery, decorated with circular openings within arched recesses.

At the top is a taller clearstory with pointed arches fronting a wall-passage. The architecture shows signs of having been modified as work progressed – for example, the clearstory arcade next to the presbytery has five arches whereas the others have only three – and the circular openings also appear to have been altered. Behind these openings was a storage space reached from the clearstory, which in turn was reached by a spiral stair in the north-west corner of the transept.

Left: The north transept, the most complete part of the abbey church, still standing to its full height, with much of its decorative carving almost intact.

EXPLORE

The two eastern chapels each contained an altar and have rib-and-panel vaulting, with great carved keystones, or bosses, holding the moulded ribs together. One of the bosses depicts Christ in Majesty with one hand raised, blessing his flock, while a book is held in the other. A piscina serving the altar in the north chapel still survives in its east wall. The two chapels differ in size. The inner chapel is two bays deep with arches opening into the presbytery; the outer one is one bay deep with an arch opening into the transept. Holes can be seen cut into the masonry: these would have held fixings for wooden screens enclosing the chapels.

When the abbey was abandoned by the canons, these chapels were appropriated as private burial-places by notable families of the district, among them the Haliburtons and the Haigs of Bemersyde. Their most distinguished representatives, Sir Walter Scott and Earl Haig, are buried here.

The south transept mirrored the arrangement in the north transept but only the splendid south gable survives. This has a magnificent window composed of five lancets, stepped at their bases to accommodate the roof of the dormitory on the outside.

The night stair, used by the canons when going to and from their night-time services, passes through a large round-headed doorway in the west side of the gable. The smaller, lintelled doorway to its east led to what was the sacristy, but was modified when the sacristy became a private burial aisle. In the south-east corner of the transept is a small round-headed door which led down to the vestry and also gave access to a spiral stair from which the dormitory, the clearstory and the bell-chamber were reached.

Top right: A boss depicting Christ in Majesty in the vaulted ceiling of the north transept.

Above: The majestic south gable of the south transept, seen from the east.

DRYBURGH ABBEY

THE CLOISTER

The cloister was the focal point of the canons' lives when they were not taking part in church services. It was placed on the south side of the church to benefit from exposure to the sun. The abbey's domestic accommodation was arranged around a square open space known as the cloister garth.

The canons' domestic spaces lay in two ranges built along the east and south sides of the cloister, and at Dryburgh these are unusually complete and informative. The east range housed the most important spaces, including the chapter house, the warming house and the novices' day room; the south range housed the refectory and kitchen. The west side does not appear to have had a range, just an enclosing wall.

The cloister garth was bordered by a covered walkway, which sheltered the brethren from the elements. The roof along the east cloister walk was originally carried on a stone vault but this was later removed and replaced by a timber framework, mainly supported on projecting stone corbels. On the garth side was an open arcaded wall, the foundations of which have been traced. The covered walk was also used for private study: this is confirmed by a shelved book-cupboard in the east wall.

EXPLORE

THE PROCESSIONAL DOOR

The ground-floor spaces within the cloister are connected to the south aisle of the church by the east processional door. This is the only door still in use of three that linked church and cloister. The façade of the doorway faces the cloister and has an arched, semi-circular head, enriched with dogtooth ornament. The splayed sides have recessed orders with disengaged shafts, the caps of which are plain on the east side and decorated with water-leaf designs on the west.

This doorway had been removed to the mansion of Newton Don, near Kelso, before being reinstated in 1894. The grandeur of its design emphasises not only the importance of the church but also of the cloister, as part of the processional route taken by the brethren during important services.

Opposite: The south, west and north ranges of the cloister as they may have looked around 1450, with the River Tweed beyond.

Above: The processional door from the cloister into the church.

THE EAST RANGE: UPPER FLOOR

The upper floor of the east range houses the canons' dormitory. Today it can only be reached via the night-stair from the church.

It was lit from the west by a transept window featuring a carving of a bat in its left side, a nice touch of humour by one of the masons. The dormitory originally ran the whole length of the east range.

The dormitory was once accessible via a day-stair (now lost), leading from the cloister. At the south end was the latrine-block, or reredorter, flushed by the main water-channel.

The first-floor space has undergone several changes. The original roof-line is visible in the north wall, below the five-light window, and evidence of heat-cracked masonry in the transept gable suggests the original roof may have been destroyed by fire. The replacement roof seems to have been raised to the full height of the gable, perhaps to provide extra accommodation. The double tier of windows and the blocked up south transept window are clearly shown on an engraving of 1678 by the military engineer John Slezer (see page 29).

In the late 1500s, a private dwelling for the commendator, or lay abbot, was constructed within the north part of the former dormitory. This consisted of a two-storeyed house with a north wing, and was entered from a fore-stair built against the east side of the east range.

Top right: The commendator's house on the first floor of the east range, as it may have looked when in use around 1600.

Top left: The carved bat that nestles in the left-hand corner of a window at the north-west of the dormitory.

Above: Cracked masonry on the north wall of the dormitory provides evidence of fire damage.

THE EAST RANGE: GROUND FLOOR

The well-preserved ground floor of the east range contains several of the abbey's most important rooms.

The room closest to the processional door may once have been divided by a timber partition into two rooms: a library and a sacristy. A book cupboard survives from the library.

The sacristy was used to store items required for church services (for example, altar frontals and vestments). This was also where the celebrants at Mass put on their robes. Now known as St Modan's Chapel, this barrel-vaulted chamber has stone benches around its walls, and once had two exits into the south transept. It was originally lit by two windows in the east wall, but an almond-shaped window was later inserted above them. After 1786 it became a burial aisle for the Erskine family, and it is not normally accessible.

The parlour, beside the sacristy, was the only part of the abbey in which conversation was allowed. This meeting place has two aumbries (cupboards) in the south wall and may also have had timber benches along the side walls. It originally had doors at either end, so that it could be used as a passageway from the cloister to the cemetery. In the 1800s the space was appropriated as a second burial chamber by the Erskine family, and at that time the eastern doorway was built up and a window inserted. The parlour now contains a wonderful collection of carved stones from the abbey.

Top: The arched doorways of the east range.

Above: The almond-shaped window in the east wall of the sacristy.

Left: A human head, probably from a gravestone, is among the carved stones displayed in the sacristy.

THE CHAPTER HOUSE

After the church, the chapter house was the most important building in the abbey. It served as the canons' principal meeting place, and they gathered here each day to be given news and instructions and to confess their misdemeanours.

It is entered through a round-headed door decorated in much the same way as the east processional door. It is flanked by twin-light windows in a style belonging to the late 1100s. The steps down into the room are modern. The north end is quarried into the sloping ground, and the floor lies 1.5m below the level of the cloister walkway. The grand entrance and the scale of the room reflect its importance.

The chapter house has a barrel-vaulted ceiling and three windows at the east end. The canons sat on stone seats around the walls. The more elaborate blind arcading along the east wall was clearly reserved as seating for the abbot and his senior office-bearers. The upper part of the arcading has been painted with geometric patterns. The arches along the side walls were created with paint rather than costlier stone work. The white-plastered walls were also painted, with imitation jointing in red. Chevrons and other patterns survive in isolated places such as around the north window.

Archaeological excavations in 2002–06 identified a stone culvert, or water channel, running around three sides of the chapter house, and the corner of a building possibly associated with the abbey cemetery, perhaps an infirmary.

Above: Surviving medieval paintwork in the chapter house.

Left: The chapter house as it may have looked when fully decorated.

THE WARMING HOUSE AND THE NOVICES' DAY ROOM

In the south-east corner of the cloister, a stair leads down from the middle terrace to the lowest terrace and the other rooms of the east range. The door at the top of the stair was secured by a timber draw-bar: its slot is visible in the west side.

To the south of the chapter house, the warming house, or calefactory, was a room in which the canons could enjoy the comfort of a fire. The space was once covered by an elegant rib-vault carried on central pillars and slender corbels. In the 1300s, a hooded fireplace was built in the centre of the west wall, its corbels carved with foliate patterns, one depicting oak leaves and acorns. Also around this time the windows were enlarged to improve the lighting of the room. In the south-east corner is a small mural closet. In the 1700s the warming house was apparently used as a cow byre.

Separated from the warming house by a barrel-vaulted passage, or slype, is the novices' day room, where new members received instruction from the novice master. This space resembles the earlier warming house, with a fireplace in the east wall and the original window form.

Top left: The large, east-facing windows of the warming house.

Top centre: The remains of what was once a large fireplace in the warming house.

Top right: The novices' day room, where new members of the order received their training.

THE SOUTH RANGE

The south range housed the abbey's refectory, or dining room, along with associated storage space. Although less well preserved than the east range, it still has its magnificent rose window.

Refectories were often raised above the level of the cloister, perhaps as a reminder of the upper room in which Christ took his last supper with his disciples. At Dryburgh, the refectory is elevated above a basement, which was originally rib-vaulted although barrel vaults were inserted in the 1400s. These vaults provided storage for food and wine. An arched recess in the south-west corner of the cloister may represent the washing place, known as a lavatory, where the canons washed their hands before eating.

The refectory was presumably entered from the cloister towards its west end, and the space was lit by a series of windows in the north and south walls and by the very fine twelve-petal rose window high up in the west gable. This rose window, the only survivor of this group, is very similar to the rose

Top: The rose window on the west gable of the south range.

Above: The rose window at Jedburgh Abbey, whose design is remarkably similar.

Right: A cutaway illustration shows the south and east ranges of the cloister as they may have looked around 1450. The refectory is shown at the bottom left, with storage vaults below.

EXPLORE

window adorning Jedburgh Abbey's church, which was installed in the 1400s. The refectory's high table would have been at the east end, probably accompanied by a pulpit from which one of the brethren would read during meals.

West of the refectory were the kitchens, and between the two was a servery, divided from the refectory by a screen. Below the servery was a passage from the cloister to the kitchen. The doorway from the cloister bears the arms of John Stewart, a commendator of the abbey in the 1550s, and below it a stone incised with B (for Buchan) and the date 1788.

THE WATER CHANNEL AND GATEHOUSE

South of the cloister was the main water channel, filled with water drawn from the Tweed. On its south bank is a small gatehouse, built in the 1500s. This was at one time connected to the main buildings by a covered bridge but only the lower part of the bridge now survives. The gatehouse bears heraldic shields carved on its skewputts. Further to the south is a stone obelisk erected by the Earl of Buchan in 1794 (see page 21).

Top: The coat of arms of John Stewart, who was commendator of the abbey in the 1550s.

Above: The gatehouse added at the south-west corner of the abbey complex in the 1500s.

Right: One of the gatehouse's carved skewputts.

THE HISTORY OF
DRYBURGH ABBEY

Founded around 1150 by Hugh de Moreville, as part of the royal patronage of church reform, Dryburgh Abbey was home to a community of Premonstratensian canons. It was the first and largest of six monasteries established by the order in Scotland.

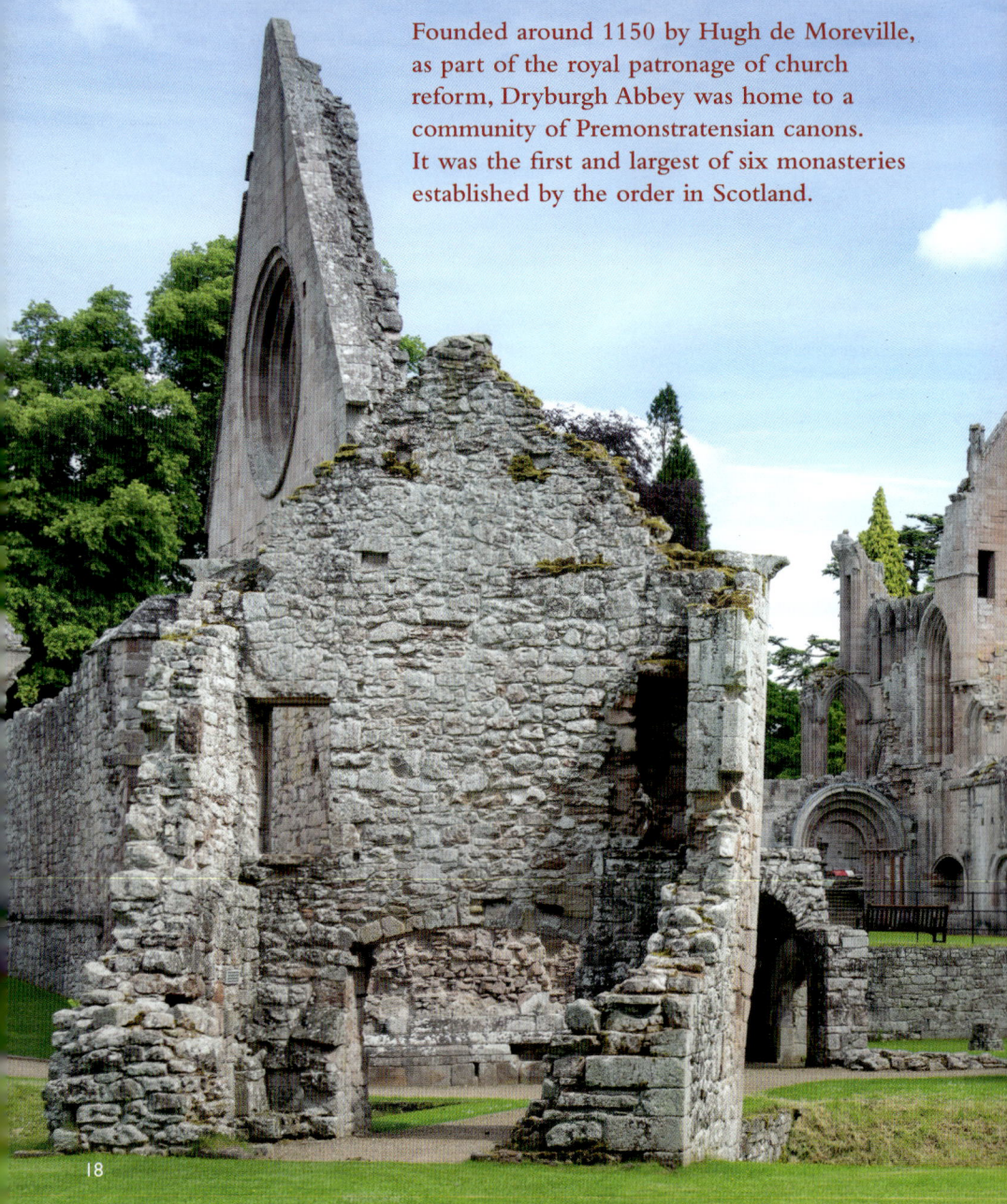

HISTORY

Although peaceful and secluded, the abbey could not escape altogether from the conflict of the secular world. It was damaged by passing armies during the medieval period and its canons were often occupied by disputes in the land-courts.

The area suffered repeatedly during Border warfare. The abbey was burned twice in the 1300s and at least once in the 1500s. After the attack of 1544 left the great abbey in ruins, its commendators built a new house within the shell of the canons' former dormitory.

In 1786, the abbey was bought by the 11th Earl of Buchan, who transformed it as the focus of an extensive designed landscape, which he entitled 'The Temple of Caledonian Fame'.

DRYBURGH ABBEY

THE ABBEY'S FOUNDATION

Dryburgh Abbey was established in 1150 by white-clad Premonstratensian canons. They were invited to this idyllic spot from Alnwick, Northumberland, by Hugh de Moreville, Constable of Scotland and Lord of Lauderdale.

This was against the background of a period of religious revival and generous royal piety which began with Malcolm III and Margaret, his queen, in the late 11th century and reached its peak during the reign of their sixth and youngest son, David I (1124–53). Through the munificence of David and his associates, the majority of Scotland's abbeys and priories were established, and Dryburgh was among them.

Hugh de Moreville, of Anglo-Norman descent, had befriended David in England and had come north at his invitation. He had led an active military career in support of his king's political ambitions. He had been granted extensive estates in the eastern Borders – chiefly Lauderdale but also along the Tweed at places like Newton Don and Dryburgh – as well as the whole of Cunningham, the northern part of Ayrshire. He also held land at Bozeat, in Northamptonshire, in King David's English Honour of Huntingdon. His marriage to Beatrice de Beauchamp linked him with the greatest landowner in Bedfordshire. By the time Dryburgh Abbey was founded, Hugh was constable of Scotland and one of the most powerful men in the country.

Top: The Eildon Hills dominate the landscape to the north-west of Dryburgh.

Above left: An illustration of David I, based on a depiction in a contemporary document.

HISTORY

Hugh's motivation in founding the abbey remains a mystery but, in a time when religious belief permeated almost every aspect of everyday life, the need to atone for past sins and thus avoid a terrible fate in the afterlife was a very real one. Founding an abbey, despite the huge personal expense, would have represented an act of special generosity to the cause of spiritual regeneration. It also demonstrated Hugh's standing in society, and allowed for a perpetual round of prayers to be offered up to God for his soul and those of his family. Hugh was evidently committed to his foundation for in his old age he enrolled as a novice at the abbey, and he died there in 1162.

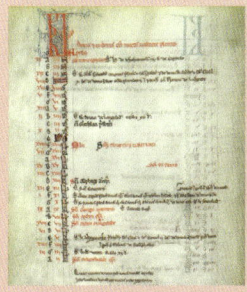

Left: An English Calendar of Saints dating from the 1200s.

Left: The carving of James I on the obelisk's east face.

ST MODAN THE MISSIONARY

A medieval Calendar of Scottish Saints (similar to the English one shown above) records that the abbey's location is associated with St Modan. The quiet seclusion of Dryburgh may seem an ideal setting for the home of an early Christian missionary and therefore this account is plausible. In common with many figures from the early Christian period, Modan's life is shrouded in mystery. He is thought to have lived in the late 500s and early 600s, and to have been a follower of St Columba. He is linked with Falkirk and Rosneath, in Dunbartonshire, as well as Dryburgh. However, no tangible evidence has been discovered at Dryburgh to support this literary information.

THE OBELISK

In the late 1700s, the ruins of the abbey were bought by David Steuart Erskine, the 11th Earl of Buchan. He had a deep interest in the history of the Scottish nation, and set about making the abbey the focus of a 'Temple of Caledonian Fame'. One of the new monuments he placed in the grounds is an obelisk, set up to the south of the refectory in 1794 to commemorate the abbey's founder, Hugh de Moreville, who is represented in low relief on the side facing the abbey. Representations of James I and James II were added later by Buchan's heir, Sir David Erskine.

DRYBURGH ABBEY

THE EARLY YEARS OF THE ABBEY

Hugh de Moreville and his wife Beatrice were the abbey's greatest benefactors, liberally bestowing churches and lands from their extensive estates. Gifts also came from King David I, including the church in Lanark, and from other great landowners, such as the de Vauxs of Dirleton, in East Lothian, who gave the island of Fidra to the canons in 1220.

Much of what is recorded about the early years of the abbey comes from its cartulary, or register book. The focus of this document was the abbey's business affairs, so it is not surprising that it offers the impression of a community accumulating lands and often quarrelling over them.

The work of constructing the great abbey church and of replacing the first temporary quarters of the canons with more permanent ranges of buildings is not mentioned in the cartulary, but the buildings themselves offer evidence of the progress of this work.

The stonemasons would have begun work on the east end of the church so that the high altar was made available to the canons at the earliest opportunity. Construction work then moved on to the lower walls of the south transept and the east range of the cloister; the east processional door and the chapter house entrance survive as wonderful examples of architecture of the late 1100s. The masons then returned to the church to complete the canons' choir; the north transept chapels and the south transept gable are elegantly constructed in the style of the early 1200s.

Top: An aerial view of the abbey from the south-west.

Right: An ornately carved basin found in the west range and possibly used for ritual cleansing. The carving style dates it to the early years of the abbey.

HISTORY

The names of Dryburgh's abbots are recorded, but none of them appears to have been particularly outstanding either as scholar or as cleric. However, they were substantial landowning lords. The third abbot, Adam, was apparently an excellent preacher and he made his reputation at Dryburgh. However, while on a visit to Prémontré he fell in love with the way of life of the Carthusian order. On his return to Britain he entered the Carthusian monastery, or charterhouse, at Witham in Somerset, where he ended his days.

The canons were permitted to serve as priests in the churches they were given, but more often they appointed vicars, or deputies, who were paid a small stipend. The lands were farmed by tenants and the rents were collected regularly. Among the canons, one name stands out, but for not for any religious reason. Brother Marcus, we are told, was suspended in 1320 for punching the abbot!

Above: The seal of the abbot of Dryburgh, dating from the 1230s.

SOURCING THE STONE

Since major medieval buildings in Scotland were built from stone, stonemasonry was among the most important crafts. Stone was generally quarried as close to the site as possible. The warm-pink sandstone used to build Dryburgh Abbey was obtained from freestone quarries situated to the north of the abbey and also on the opposite bank of the River Tweed. This local stone gives great charm to the appearance of the abbey today. Timber for roofs, floors, screens and doors would also have been obtained locally. The construction of a large church or an abbey could take many years to complete.

Right: Extracting stone from a medieval quarry.

DRYBURGH ABBEY

THE PREMONSTRATENSIANS

Dryburgh was the first Premonstratensian abbey in Scotland. The *Chronicle of Melrose* **records the arrival of the order on St Martin's Day, 1150.**

The Order of Premonstratensians, also known as the white canons from the colour of their habit, was a relatively recent establishment, set up around 1120 by St Norbert and following the rule of St Augustine, with certain modifications. The order took its name from its first seat, Prémontré, near Laon in France.

Norbert, a cleric at the court of the archbishop of Cologne, had shown little enthusiasm for the religious life until he was thrown from his horse during a thunderstorm. After retiring to a Benedictine abbey he earned the displeasure of his superiors by attempting reforms, then left and undertook an evangelising mission which eventually led him to Prémontré. Initially, he adopted the Rule of St Augustine, a guide to the conduct of canons, combining the cloistered life of the monk with the preaching role of the priest. However, he attached great importance to personal hardship and austerity, and modified the rule to this effect.

Top left: St Norbert, founder of the Premonstratensian order, as depicted by the 17th-century Flemish printmaker Cornelis Galle.

Left: A Premonstratensian canon in his white robes and hat.

HISTORY

The Premonstratensians were not monks but regular canons, that is priests who lived together in community and followed a regula, or rule. Their first foundation in England was at Newhouse, in Lincolnshire, in 1143. From there, Alnwick was founded 1147, and Dryburgh was established as a daughter house of Alnwick. Dryburgh became the premier house of the order in Scotland, although this role was disputed by Soulseat, in Galloway, founded around 1161 directly from Prémontré. There were four other Premonstratensian establishments in Scotland: Whithorn (founded around 1175), Tongland (1218) and Hollywood (by 1225) in Galloway, and Fearn (around 1225) in Ross.

Dryburgh Abbey had two daughter houses in Ireland, both in County Antrim. Carrickfergus was founded before 1183 and Drumcross by 1250. Both, ironically, suffered severely during the Scottish attack on Ulster in 1315–17, from which Carrickfergus never recovered.

Above: Whithorn Priory, a Premonstratensian establishment in the far south-west of Scotland.

Left: Alnwick Abbey in Northumberland, the second Premonstratensian foundation in England. Dryburgh Abbey was established as a daughter house of Alnwick.

THE DAILY ROUND

In medieval times, religious belief permeated almost every aspect of life. Abbeys like Dryburgh represented beacons of prayer in a sinful world, and the canons offered to God a perpetual round of prayers on behalf of those who chose to remain in the outside world, most importantly of course for the founder and his family and the abbey's other benefactors.

To achieve this, the canons spent most of their time in the abbey church. They were awakened around 1am by the dormitory bell, going into the church via the night-stair, and retired at around 8pm. Between these times they celebrated Mass, offered up private prayers and attended the eight set offices, known as 'hours'. Each morning after Prime, the second office of the day, they gathered together in the chapter house to discuss business and discipline. A proportion of their time was spent in the cloister, reading, writing and contemplating, and they gathered in the refectory for frugal meals twice a day. It was quite a small community. It appears that there may never have been many more than 20 canons resident at the abbey at any one time.

Above: The canons file past lay worshippers in the nave and into the choir beyond before celebrating Mass.

Right: A medieval canon at prayer.

HISTORY

COMMUNAL LIVING

The monastic way of life involved the canons living and worshipping together as a close-knit community. Their daily routine reinforced this bond, in which the brethren would support each other in their battles against sin. As well as the church services, talking, eating, washing and sleeping were all closely regulated. During the medieval period, a wider division developed between the abbots of abbeys and the monks or canons. At first, abbots were expected to sleep in the common dormitory, but by the time Dryburgh was founded this practice had become uncommon.

The organisation of the abbey was under the direction of the abbot and his deputy, the prior. Among the other office-bearers were the precentor, in charge of the chanting of prayers; the sacrist, who looked after the church, its furnishings and the vestments; the novice master, who instructed new recruits; the cellarer, who managed the abbey's provisions; the infirmarer, who looked after the sick and the elderly; and the almoner, who dispensed alms (charity) to the poor and needy.

Top: Canons sleeping side by side in a communal dormitory.

Right: The reconstructed night-stair in the south transept. The original stair was used by canons to access the church directly from their dormitory for night-time services.

DRYBURGH ABBEY

WAR AND PEACE

The comparative tranquility of Dryburgh was shattered during the Wars of Independence with England which erupted in 1296.

The worst disaster occurred in 1322, when an English army was retreating south, following Edward II's second unsuccessful invasion of Scotland. On reaching Dryburgh, the English forces set fire to the abbey: it seems they took a detour to wreak vengeance upon hearing the abbey bells ringing out in celebration of their defeat. A simpler explanation might be that the troops tried to obtain provisions from the abbey and, failing to do so, set fire to it. The heat-cracked masonry on the south side of the south transept may be a legacy from this attack, the first of several during the medieval period.

Above: Edward II is encouraged to invade Scotland in an illustration from the *Chronicle of England*, produced around 1310–30.

HISTORY

The destruction of the abbey seems to have prompted financial assistance from the faithful. King Robert I (the Bruce) gave financial help and Bishop John of Glasgow, in 1326, granted the abbey the church at Maxton as 'an act of piety to succour the needy'. The task of rebuilding then appears to have begun almost immediately.

The reconstruction of the dormitory in particular was on a grand scale, quite unparalleled anywhere else in Scotland. Judging by the evidence in John Slezer's engraving of 1678, the canons' new sleeping quarters rose to the full height of the south transept, giving them at least one extra floor. The replacement of the stone vault over the east cloister walk by a timber lean-to roof may also have been necessitated by this first recorded attack.

After a period of comparative peace, war returned in 1385 during Richard II's invasion. The abbey was 'devastated by hostile fire', apparently almost beyond recovery. Robert III gave financial assistance to the abbey in its work of rebuilding. Other donations around this time may also be linked to this work. They included donations from the 4th Earl of Douglas, Lord Halyburton of Dirleton and Lord Maxwell of Caerlaverock in Dumfriesshire. The rebuilding after 1385 is most evident at the west end of the church, including the west door.

Top: John Slezer's engraving of the abbey, produced in 1678, shows part of the east range of the cloister still standing four storeys high.

Bottom: Richard II of England, who personally led an invasion of Scotland in 1385. Although no significant battles were fought, Dryburgh Abbey suffered major damage.

DRYBURGH ABBEY

THE LATER YEARS

Top: A carved ceiling boss depicting St Andrew, patron saint of Scotland, added during the remodelling of the abbey in the 1400s.

Above: A window with its panes divided by Y-shaped tracery, also added in the 1400s.

Monastic life continued at Dryburgh despite the drastic effects of war. However, the abbey was to face other kinds of disruptions.

As early as the mid-1300s the abbot received special powers from Rome to deal with indiscipline, a sign that the community's austere life was being eroded. There were further disputes throughout the 1400s: the canons seem to have been more intent on defending their earthly possessions in the land-courts than on pursuing their spiritual duties. This was a time of deepening disrespect for the monastic orders. By the early 1500s there were growing calls for reform.

One scandal was the misuse of church appointments. Commendators were secular officials, originally appointed to collect the revenues of an abbey when the abbot's post lay vacant. But the system began to be abused. Dryburgh received its first commendator, Andrew Forman, in 1507. He scarcely visited, merely drawing his income and leaving the prior to run the abbey.

David Hamilton, Bishop of Argyll, was commendator from 1518 until his death in 1522, not long before war returned to the Borders. The impact on Dryburgh is not recorded, but it seems unlikely that the abbey escaped the Earl of Surrey's raids.

The next appointment was carried out in a way which sheds light on ecclesiastical patronage at this time. Regent Albany, governing Scotland on behalf of the young James V, bestowed the commendatorship of Dryburgh on a minor, John Stewart, son of the Earl of Lennox. It was then transferred to James Stewart, a kinsman, in return for a generous pension. Some building work may have been carried out at this time, for John Stewart's coat of arms can be seen in the south range.

HISTORY

On his death in 1541, James Stewart was succeeded by Thomas Erskine, second son of Lord Erskine, after which the abbey remained in Erskine hands. In 1544 the abbey was raided again, this time by the Earl of Hertford. A contemporary English writer described how, on 4 November 1544, 700 men 'rode into Scotland upon the water of Tweide to a town called Dryburgh with an abbey in the same, which was a pretty town and well buylded; and they burnte the same town and abbey, saving the churche ...' Neither the abbey nor the town was rebuilt.

In 1560, Scotland's Parliament adopted the Protestant Confession of Faith, forbidding the celebration of Mass and abolishing papal authority over the Church. In many places this led to extensive destruction. At Dryburgh, the commendator, David Erskine, the sub-prior and the eight remaining canons embraced the reformed religion, and were allowed to remain. However, no new members were permitted.

By this time the cloister buildings must have been in disrepair, and the construction of a new commendator's house in the shell of the dormitory, a vaulted range against the outside of the west cloister wall and the gatehouse may reflect a dispersed community, with the canons living in individual plots. By 1580 their numbers had fallen to four and by 1584 to two. In 1600 a document signed by the commendator noted: 'all the convent thairof [are] now deceissit'.

Top: The coat of arms of Thomas Howard, 2nd Earl of Surrey, who raided the Border abbeys in 1523.

Centre: Edward Seymour, 2nd Earl of Hertford, who raided Dryburgh Abbey in 1544.

Bottom: John Erskine, 1st Earl of Mar, who became commendator of Dryburgh Abbey in 1547.

BUCHAN'S ROMANTIC RUIN

In the 1700s, the ivy-clad ruins of the abbey attracted the attention of David Erskine, 11th Earl of Buchan. A descendant of the Erskine commendators of Dryburgh and the chief founder of the Society of Antiquaries of Scotland in 1780, Buchan purchased Dryburgh House and set about creating a charming landscape, in which the ancient abbey figured prominently.

Buchan spent a great deal of time and money recording the religious houses of Scotland and researching their origins. He was also a member of the movement which advocated the retention of ruins as elegant reminders of our glorious past. During the 40 years he spent at Dryburgh House he created a magnificent garden, planted specimen trees and built classical follies. He also preserved the ruins of the great abbey, making it the most magnificent of garden ornaments. He planted a variety of parkland trees which can still be seen here, and as well as planting shrubs in the cloister, he erected 'a statue of Inigo Jones in the centre of the quadrangle which will have a fine effect in one of the views'.

Above: David Steuart Erskine, 11th Earl of Buchan, who purchased Dryburgh House and subsequently transformed the abbey ruins.

Above: The obelisk at the south of the site was erected by the 11th Earl, though the carvings of James I and James II (pictured) were added later.

HISTORY

Left: The elaborate garden created by the earl in the cloister garden, with its statue of the architect Inigo Jones.

Below: The earl's gravestone in the sacristy.

Like most antiquarians of his time, Buchan was unable to resist the temptation to meddle, and the abbey ruins are full of oddities attributable to him. These include the inscription 'Hic jacet Archibald' cut into the wall beside the chapter house entrance, and the re-erected grave-slabs around the walls of the presbytery. One of the most curious features of his work is his obelisk to the south of the gatehouse (see page 21).

Buchan also undertook excavations, and on discovering a stone coffin he opened it and removed a chalice (with the finger bones of the poor occupant still attached), a crook and part of a silk shroud. Despite what would now be considered inappropriate interventions, it is largely thanks to him that so much of the abbey survives. When he died in 1829, he was laid to rest in the sacristy, which he had appropriated as the family burial vault.

A SECLUDED LANDSCAPE

The abbey's peaceful riverside location and carefully landscaped grounds offer a haven for a variety of birds and wild flowers. Many of the majestic trees that frame the abbey's ruins were planted during the 1700s, and the Dryburgh Yew (left), to the east of the abbey's east range, is considered to be among the most important trees in Scotland.

SIR WALTER SCOTT

'Never, on any occasion, was there beheld more intense feeling than when the remains of this worthy man passed through the villages and hamlets, the inhabitants of which were, in general, in mourning and standing uncovered.'

James Morton, *The Monastic Annals of Teviotdale*, 1832

One of the great men to lie entombed within the abbey is Sir Walter Scott. Among the most influential writers of the 1800s, he is probably most renowned as the founder of the historical novel genre.

Through his writing, Scott transformed the image of Scotland, both at home and overseas. He was also active in Scottish political life. His grave is in the north transept chapel he referred to as St Mary's Aisle, his *domus ultimus* ('final home'), which had been appropriated by his family after the Reformation. Scott was buried at Dryburgh by right of his ancestors, the Haliburtons of Newmains. Robert Haliburton, great-uncle to Sir Walter Scott, had sold the abbey following his bankruptcy.

Scott himself wrote, 'We have nothing left of Dryburgh, although my father's maternal inheritance, but the right of stretching our bones where mine may perhaps be laid ere any eye but my own glances over these pages.' He was laid to rest on 26 September 1832, amid great ceremony.

It is ironic that Buchan and Scott should be buried so close together, for Buchan was vilified late in life by Scott, who succeeded in ruining his reputation.

Top: An illustration of Sir Walter Scott's funeral at the abbey in 1832.

Right: Scott's grave in the north transept.

HISTORY

EARL HAIG AND AFTER

Far left: A portrait of Earl Haig by the prominent artist John Singer Sargent.

Left: Haig's grave in the abbey grounds.

Field Marshal Earl Douglas Haig of Bemersyde, buried close by Scott's grave in 1928, was commander-in-chief of the British Expeditionary Forces in France and Flanders during World War I.

Douglas Haig had a distinguished, yet controversial, military career, and after the war he served as commander-in-chief of the British Home Forces until 1921. On retirement, he dedicated himself to service in the Royal British Legion, which he had helped to establish. He was granted the title Earl of Bemersyde in memory of his ancestors, who originated from the district of La Hague in Normandy, had crossed to England in 1066 and who settled at Bemersyde, a short distance up the hill from Dryburgh, as vassals of Hugh de Moreville, the founder of the abbey.

The abbey has been in the care of the State since 1919, and work began soon after that date to consolidate the upstanding masonry. The work of carefully maintaining and conserving the abbey's historic fabric for the benefit of future generations continues today, along with archaeological investigation, when opportunities allow, that adds to our knowledge of the site.

For today's visitors to Dryburgh Abbey, its graceful ruins, nestling in their picturesque setting beside the River Tweed, offer echoes of the monastic way of life that flourished here for over 400 years. Perhaps it is easy to imagine why the contemplative life of a medieval canon at Dryburgh was so attractive.

DISCOVER HISTORIC SCOTLAND

Dryburgh Abbey is one of a dozen Historic Scotland properties in the Borders, a selection of which is shown below.

JEDBURGH ABBEY
Founded around 1138 by King David I, Jedburgh has withstood centuries of border warfare to survive as a magnificent example of medieval architecture.

↗ In Jedburgh, on the A68
🕐 Open all year
📞 01835 863925
🚗 Approx 12 miles from Dryburgh Abbey

MELROSE ABBEY
Established in 1136 as a modest Cistercian monastery, Melrose Abbey was destroyed by Richard II in 1385, but much of its magnificent replacement survives.

↗ In Melrose, off the A7 or A68
🕐 Open all year
📞 01896 822562
🚗 Approx 8 miles from Dryburgh Abbey

SMAILHOLM TOWER
Built as a tower-house for the Pringles around 1430, remote Smailholm has survived reiving and the 'Rough Wooing' to retain its spectacular charm.

↗ In Smailholm village, north of Jedburgh on the A6089
🕐 Open all year
   Winter: open weekends only
📞 01573 460365
🚗 Approx 6 miles from Dryburgh Abbey

HERMITAGE CASTLE
Isolated and intimidating, Hermitage dominated Liddesdale for centuries, witnessing bloody violence, treasonable pacts and a royal romantic tryst.

↗ Near Newcastleton on the B6399
🕐 Open summer only
📞 01387 376222
🚗 Approx 40 miles from Dryburgh Abbey

For more information on all Historic Scotland sites, go to www.historicenvironment.scot/visit-a-place

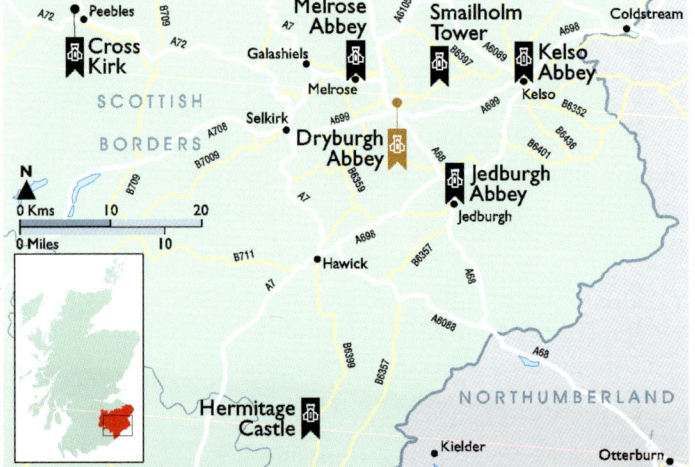

Symbol key	
Car parking	P
Bus parking	🚌
Reasonable wheelchair access	♿
Toilets	🚻
Interpretive display	
Shop	🎁
Picnic area	
Visitor centre	
Bicycle parking	🚲
May close for lunch	🕐
Accessible by public transport	
Tea/coffee facilities	
Strong footwear recommended	👟